Daily Activity Bank

PEARSON
Scott Foresman

Editorial Offices: Glenview, Illinois • Parsippany, New Jersey • New York, New York
Sales Offices: Parsippany, New Jersey • Duluth, Georgia • Glenview, Illinois • Coppell, Texas • Ontario, California

www.sfsocialstudies.com

Contents

ISBN 0-328-03926-8

11 12 13 14 V008 10 09 08 07

Fast Fact 1

Iceland's capital, Reykjavik, is the northernmost capital city in the world.

What is the northernmost major city in the continental United States?

Geography

History

Fast Fact 2

Around 1491 a mudslide buried an entire Native American village in what is now the state of Washington. It was rediscovered in 1991 after some tourists found artifacts on the beach.

What was happening along the Atlantic coast of North America in the late 1400s?

Fast Fact 3

E Pluribus Unum (Latin for *out of many, one*) is one of six inscriptions required on every coin minted by the United States.

What are the other five inscriptions?

Economics

Government
Citizenship

Fast Fact 4

The Library of Congress has on display, both online and in the Library, the oldest known map of Manhattan, drawn in 1639.

Who owned Manhattan in 1639?

Fast Fact 5

Horses aren't originally from the Americas; the Spanish introduced them in 1532.

How did the introduction of horses change the way the Cheyenne lived?

Culture

Geography

Fast Fact 6

The Atlantic Ocean is about half the size of the Pacific Ocean.

What are three islands located in the Atlantic Ocean?

Fast Fact 7

Rock drawings found on the walls of a cave in southeastern France are the earliest cave art ever discovered, dating back to 29,000 B.C.

The Anasazi drew rock art on the walls of their villages. Where would you find Anasazi rock drawings?

History

Economics

Fast Fact 8

In the 1700s, a boy as young as eight could apprentice himself for four to seven years, without pay, to learn a craft.

What were some careers in the 1700s?

Fast Fact 9

The Liberty Bell was hung in 1753, and the last time the Liberty Bell rang was on February 23, 1846, for George Washington's birthday celebration.

Name three other symbols of the United States.

Government Citizenship

Culture

Fast Fact 10

The largest ancient mound at Cahokia, Illinois, is bigger at the base than the Great Pyramid of Egypt.

Which Native Americans built large structures before the arrival of the Europeans?

Fast Fact 11

Pueblo communities joined together in 1680 and successfully drove the Spaniards out of their villages.

What do we now call the place where the Pueblo Revolt of 1680 took place?

Geography

History

Fast Fact 12

People in Japan were recycling paper as early as the year 1035.

What are some other items besides paper that can be recycled?

Fast Fact 13

The United States Mint is producing a series of quarters with a design for each state on the reverse of each coin.

What image is on the front side of each quarter?

Economics

Government Citizenship

Fast Fact 14

Legislation approved on July 30, 1956, made *In God We Trust* the national motto of the United States.

What is the motto of your state?

Fast Fact 15

The city of Tenochtitlan was founded in 1325.

Who lived at Tenochtitlan?

Culture

Geography

Fast Fact 16

Frigid Antarctica is home to the largest desert in the world.

Name a desert in the southwestern United States.

Fast Fact 17

The Inca Empire, in what is now Peru, rose to power around the year 1200.

Who defeated the Inca?

History

Economics

Fast Fact 18

The first United States commemorative coin was minted in 1892 and featured Christopher Columbus.

What is the difference between a commemorative coin and a circulating coin?

Fast Fact 19

Members of Congress cannot be arrested, except for treason or for a felony, while Congress is in session.

What are the two houses of Congress?

Government Citizenship

Culture

Fast Fact 20

Marco Polo brought many exciting inventions back to Europe from his travels in China, including the use of coal as fuel.

What else is part of our lives today that originally came from China?

Fast Fact 21

Mt. Everest is the highest mountain in the world.

What is the highest mountain in the United States, and where is it located?

Geography

History

Fast Fact 22

The Massachusetts Minutemen got their name because they could be ready to fight with just a minute's notice.

In what war were the Minutemen prepared to fight?

Fast Fact 23

To get to work, fewer people in New York City drive than use public transportation.

What are some forms of public transportation in your community?

Economics

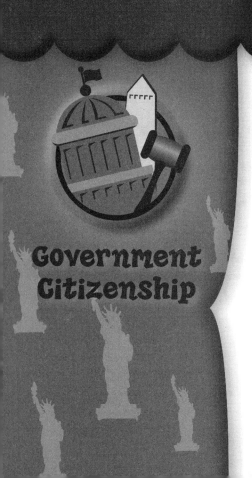

Government Citizenship

Fast Fact 24

The United States Mint is issuing new state quarters in the order that each state ratified the Constitution and was admitted to the Union.

When did your state join the Union?

Fast Fact 25

The first bar chocolate was introduced in the 1840s. Before then, people drank chocolate.

Who introduced Hernando Cortés to chocolate?

Culture

Geography

Fast Fact 26

Alaska's climate is so cold that people play golf on the frozen Bering Sea every March.

What country is across the Bering Sea from Alaska?

Fast Fact 27

Wyoming allowed women to vote when it was still a territory, and it became the first state to permit women to vote.

In what year were women throughout the United States granted the right to vote?

History

Economics

Fast Fact 28

Tobacco was first introduced in Europe in 1565. In 1604, King James I of England wrote a book attacking the new fashion of smoking.

Where was this tobacco grown?

Fast Fact 29

To be President of the United States, a person must be 35 years old, have lived in the country for fourteen years, and have been born in the United States.

Who was President of the United States before our current president?

Government Citizenship

Culture

Fast Fact 30

During *Ramadan*, the ninth month of the Islamic year, Muslims fast between dawn and sunset each day.

What is another holiday that lasts for longer than one day?

Fast Fact 31

The widest waterfall in the world is Khone Falls, which stretches for almost seven miles along the Cambodian border with Laos.

What is the name of a famous waterfall between Lake Erie and Lake Ontario?

Geography

History

Fast Fact 32

Britain first used its new colony of Australia, which was then called New South Wales, as a prison colony.

What United States colony was founded as a home for British prisoners?

Fast Fact 33

In 1760, a wampum factory was opened in New Jersey. The factory produced these shells as currency for trade with Native American groups and among the colonists.

Who is responsible for determining what may be issued as legal currency?

Economics

Government
Citizenship

Fast Fact 34

A person must be a United States citizen and at least 30 years old to run for the Senate.

Who are the United States senators from your state?

Fast Fact 35

Through the early 1800s the Seminole welcomed runaway slaves. Now there are many Black Seminoles.

Why were the Seminole able to take in the runaways?

Culture

Geography

Fast Fact 36

The Nile River in Africa is more than four thousand miles long. It would almost stretch from New York to Los Angeles and back if it flowed across the United States.

What is the longest river in the United States?

Fast Fact 37

Paul Revere's metals company once supplied the United States Mint with rolled copper for the production of early coins.

For what other patriotic act is Paul Revere famous?

History

Economics

Fast Fact 38

George Washington's plantation, Mount Vernon, was so large it had a private dock for shipping crops to market.

Who planted and harvested these crops?

Fast Fact 39

The famed cherry trees of Washington, D.C., were originally planted as a gift from the people of Tokyo, Japan, in 1912.

The Statue of Liberty was a gift to the United States from the people of which country?

Government Citizenship

Culture

Fast Fact 40

Christmas trees were originally a German tradition, brought to North America by German immigrants as early as the 1600s.

What is your favorite holiday tradition?

Fast Fact 41

Tall Trees Grove in Redwood National Park is home to the Nugget Tree, which is 365 feet tall and may be as many as 1,500 years old.

Where is Redwood National Park?

Geography

History

Fast Fact 42

During WWII, hundreds of spies parachuted behind enemy lines. One of their tools was an escape map printed with invisible ink on a handkerchief.

What materials can be used to make a parachute?

Fast Fact 43

A $2.50 gold piece was a standard coin in the United States in the early 1800s.

What coins are currently in circulation?

Economics

Government Citizenship

Fast Fact 44

No member of the House of Representatives can represent more than 30,000 people.

How many representatives does your state have in the House of Representatives?

Fast Fact 45

More pitchers have been named to the National Baseball Hall of Fame than right fielders, shortstops, or left fielders.

In what country was baseball first played?

Culture

Geography

Fast Fact 46

Prudhoe Bay is the largest oil field in North America, at its peak pumping two million barrels of crude oil a day.

In what state is Prudhoe Bay located?

Fast Fact 47

In 1979 Susan B. Anthony became the first woman honored by the United States on a circulating coin.

Who is the only other woman to be featured on a circulating coin?

History

Economics

Fast Fact 48

After the Revolutionary War, the national government took over the debt of the various states. The new country had a national debt of more than $70 million.

What did Shays's Rebellion have to do with state debt?

Fast Fact 49

The United States population in 1790 was almost 4 million people. The 1990 census, taken exactly 200 years later, counted about 250 million people.

What is the census used for?

Government Citizenship

Culture

Fast Fact 50

Fourth of July celebrations didn't become a tradition until after the War of 1812.

Why is July 4 an important date?

Fast Fact 51

New Jersey is a small state, but it played a big role in the American Revolution.

What is a famous Revolutionary War battle that took place in New Jersey?

Geography

Fast Fact 52

The Mohawk Indians belonged to the Iroquois League, also known as the Iroquois Confederacy.

What other Native American groups belonged to the Iroquois League?

Fast Fact 53

The Delaware state quarter shows Ceasar Rodney riding to vote in favor of signing the Declaration of Independence. His vote was the tie-breaker.

Who was the first person to sign the Declaration of Independence?

Economics

Government
Citizenship

Fast Fact 54

Ben Franklin's son William served as Royal Governor of New Jersey and was imprisoned as a Loyalist during the Revolutionary War.

How did Benjamin Franklin help found our nation's government?

Fast Fact 55

George Washington had only one remaining tooth when he was inaugurated. He didn't smile often because his false teeth were uncomfortable.

What were George Washington's false teeth made of?

Culture

Geography

Fast Fact 56

The first lighthouse built by the United States is still standing in Virginia Beach, Virginia. Shifting sand once filled the kitchen to the ceiling.

This lighthouse, called Old Cape Henry, helped guide ships on what body of water?

Fast Fact 57

When George Washington was elected President, there was a king in France and an emperor in China. Neither France nor China has such a position today.

What are some other titles, past and present, for a leader of a country?

History

Economics

Fast Fact 58

By 1619 tobacco was so valuable in Virginia that it was used as money.

What official types of money did people use in the United States immediately after the Revolutionary War?

Fast Fact 59

The original Constitution of the United States document is stored in the National Archives building in Washington, D.C., in a vault with doors that weigh 10,000 pounds.

When was the Constitution of the United States ratified?

Government Citizenship

Culture

Fast Fact 60

The Vietnamese New Year celebration is known as *Tet*. Instead of counting individual birthdays, everyone turns one year older on this day.

What are two things you like to do to celebrate the new year?

Fast Fact 61

In the 1770s Jean Baptiste Pointe Du Sable, a fur trader, founded a trading post on the southwestern shore of Lake Michigan.

What major Midwestern city did this outpost later become?

Geography

History

Fast Fact 62

In 1800 John and Abigail Adams moved into the mansion that would become known as the White House. It was brand new and entirely unfurnished.

What is one other fact you know about President Adams?

Fast Fact 63

Starting in the 1860s, steamboats could carry immigrants from Europe to America in only ten days. Sailing ships at that time took at least a month.

What American engineer developed the first commercially successful steam-powered riverboat?

Economics

Government
Citizenship

Fast Fact 64

Thomas Jefferson loved vanilla ice cream so much that he brought a recipe for it from France to America in the late 1770s. The Library of Congress has this handwritten recipe.

Where is the Library of Congress located?

Fast Fact 65

Customs vary from culture to culture. Many people from Asian, Latin, and Caribbean cultures avoid eye contact to show respect.

What are two things you do in order to show respect?

Culture

Geography

Fast Fact 66

Grand Coulee Dam is three times larger than the Great Pyramid of Egypt. It is the largest concrete dam in the United States and provides the most water power.

The Grand Coulee Dam is located on what river?

Fast Fact 67

Dolley Madison rescued a portrait of George Washington and one of herself from a fire at the White House. The fire was set by the British.

During what war did this attack occur?

History

Economics

Fast Fact 68

People were amazed when New York Governor DeWitt Clinton wanted to build a canal across New York State. They called it "Clinton's Folly."

How did the Erie Canal, which was finished in 1825, improve trade between New York City and the Midwest?

Fast Fact 69

The town of Peterborough, New Hampshire, opened the first free public library in the United States in 1833.

What sort of items can you check out at your closest library?

Government Citizenship

Culture

Fast Fact 70

The most famous sled-dog race in the world is called the Iditarod. Each year, many people compete in this 1,100-mile race between Anchorage and Nome, Alaska.

What is a popular sport played by people in your state?

Fast Fact 71

The earthquakes that struck New Madrid, Missouri, during the winter of 1811–1812 changed the course of the Mississippi River.

What states border Missouri?

Geography

History

Fast Fact 72

Once the United States Navy commissions a ship, it is considered active until it is decommissioned, or retired.

What is the oldest active United States Navy warship?

Fast Fact 73

The Erie Canal, which connected the East Coast with the Midwest, helped make New York City the largest city in the country.

After 1865, what form of transportation weakened the importance of the Erie Canal?

Economics

Fast Fact 74

Before he died, Thomas Jefferson wrote the inscription for his own tombstone, listing his achievements in life. He didn't mention that he had served as President of the United States.

What were some of Thomas Jefferson's other achievements?

Fast Fact 75

In 1950 the San Francisco 49ers became a major-league professional football team on the West Coast.

How did the name 49ers originate?

Culture

Fast Fact 76

Jackson, Mississippi, named after Andrew Jackson, is one of four state capitals named after presidents.

What are the other three state capitals named after presidents?

Fast Fact 77

A telegraph message traveled 100 million times faster than a horse or a ship.

What is the name of the language used by the telegraph?

History

Economics

Fast Fact 78

The U.S. Bureau of Engraving and Printing makes almost 37 million pieces of paper currency every day.

What does the U.S. Mint make?

Fast Fact 79

The U.S. Census did not gather employment information until 1820. There were about 350,000 people working in factories that year.

Why might the government want to gather this type of information?

Government Citizenship

Culture

Fast Fact 80

Kwanzaa, which has been celebrated in the U.S. since 1966, is a holiday honoring ancient African cultures.

The word *Kwanzaa* comes from what language?

Fast Fact 81

In 1826 a trip from Albany, New York, to Buffalo, New York, took ten days traveling on the Erie Canal.

How far is it from Albany to Buffalo?

Geography

History

Fast Fact 82

Westward, ho! wasn't just an American trend. From 1820 to 1880 about ten million people immigrated to the United States from northern and western Europe.

Name one state that joined the Union during each decade of this expansion.

Fast Fact 83

Mill girls at Lowell, Massachusetts, earned between $2.00 and $3.50 per week. As much as half of that went to the boarding houses in which they were required to live.

What are some of the technological advances that made the Lowell factories possible?

Economics

Government Citizenship

Fast Fact 84

Martin Van Buren was the first president born a United States citizen.

Who were the presidents before Van Buren?

Fast Fact 85

Clark, South Dakota, holds a Potato Days festival every summer, complete with potato sculpture contests.

Why might a town celebrate one particular food like this?

Culture

Geography

Fast Fact 86

In 1841 the first wagon train traveled overland to California, heading west from Independence, Missouri.

What are the names of the three famous wagon trails that originated in Independence, Missouri?

Fast Fact 87

Angelina and Sarah Grimké were famous women who spoke out publicly against slavery in the 1840s.

Who are two other women who became well known in the 1840s for their views on slavery?

History

Economics

Fast Fact 88

The U.S. Mint makes money making money! A quarter costs only a few pennies to make. The profit helps pay for government services such as education and defense.

How else does the government get the money to provide these services?

Fast Fact 89

Franklin Pierce installed the first central heating system and the first bathroom with hot and cold water in the White House.

How many presidents had lived in the White House by the time Franklin Pierce became president in 1853?

Government Citizenship

Culture

Fast Fact 90

The one-room schoolhouse hasn't gone away entirely. In Pennsylvania alone, more than 3,000 Amish children attend about 100 schools.

About how many students is that per school?

Fast Fact 91

Iowa is the only state with eastern and western borders created entirely by rivers.

What rivers border Iowa?

Geography

History

Fast Fact 92

In the 1850s Congress made money available to import camels to transport military supplies in the Southwest. The camels smelled awful and scared the horses, so they were sold at auction in 1866.

Who was president in 1866?

Fast Fact 93

According to the Federal Reserve, a $1 bill has an expected life of almost two years. A $20 bill should last about four years, but it is made of exactly the same materials.

Why might a $20 bill last longer than a $1 bill?

Economics

Fast Fact 94

California's state flag is based on the homemade flag flown by American settlers who took over the Mexican fort in Sonoma, California, in 1846.

What state was part of Mexico before it became an independent country, and later a state?

Fast Fact 95

There are ten national holidays in the United States. Christmas marks a religious holiday, and one holiday honors all of our Presidents.

Name five more national holidays.

Culture

Geography

Fast Fact 96

The Great Lakes hold about 95 percent of the fresh water in the United States.

Name the Great Lakes, from west to east.

Fast Fact 97

If all the gold suspended in the oceans were mined, there would be enough to give each person on Earth nine pounds.

Where was gold discovered in 1848?

History

Economics

Fast Fact 98

Elizabeth Blackwell was rejected by 29 medical schools before being accepted to Geneva Medical College in 1848. She became the first woman in the country to receive a medical degree.

A person with a medical degree might do what kind of work?

Fast Fact 99

United States currency is printed on paper specially designed by the Bureau of Engraving and Printing, with ink made using a secret formula.

What are some reasons special inks and paper are used to print money?

Government Citizenship

Culture

Fast Fact 100

Since 1969 the people of Spivey's Corner, North Carolina, have held a National Hollerin' Contest every June.

What are some festivals that you have attended?

Fast Fact 101

The highest point in Pennsylvania is lower than the lowest point in Colorado.

What is the name of the mountain range that passes through Colorado?

Geography

History

Fast Fact 102

Some thirsty 49ers were forced to pay up to $100 for a glass of water on the trail to California.

What path did thousands of 49ers take through the Sierra Nevada to reach California?

Fast Fact 103

The first labor strike in the United States took place in 1776 when members of the Journeymen Printers Union went on strike.

What are some reasons workers might decide to go on strike?

Economics

Government
Citizenship

Fast Fact 104

About 60 percent of the waste produced in America is recyclable. However, less than a third of that is actually recycled.

What are two things you can do to increase the amount of trash you recycle?

Fast Fact 105

In January 1878 the first commercial switchboard opened in New Haven, Connecticut. It served 21 telephones on 8 lines and was called a *party line*.

What is your favorite way to communicate with people who live in another city?

Culture

Geography

Fast Fact 106

The brightest city on Earth, as seen from space, is Las Vegas, Nevada.

What lake near Las Vegas helps Hoover Dam generate electricity for some of those bright city lights?

Fast Fact 107

When Harriet Beecher Stowe met President Lincoln, he said, "So you're the little woman who wrote the book that made this great war!"

To what book and to what war was Lincoln referring?

History

Economics

Fast Fact 108

William H. Russell founded the Pony Express in 1860 at a cost of almost $500,000. The mail service ran for only 18 months, leaving its founder with a loss of more than $100,000.

What invention put the Pony Express out of business?

Fast Fact 109

The Constitution sets up a line of succession in case anything should happen to the president. The first two successors are the vice-president and the Speaker of the House of Representatives.

Who is the current vice-president?

Government Citizenship

Culture

Fast Fact 110

The Cincinnati Red Stockings became the first professional U.S. baseball team in 1869.

What is the name of your local baseball team?

Fast Fact 111

Ninety percent of all volcanic activity occurs in the oceans.

Name an island chain in the United States that is still being formed by volcanic activity.

Geography

History

Fast Fact 112

Many children fought in the Civil War. Ten-year-old drummer boy John Clem won fame for surviving the fierce Battle of Shiloh.

What was the average age of a Civil War soldier?

Fast Fact 113

It took fourteen years to build the Brooklyn Bridge. Until it was paid for, people had to pay a three-cent toll to cross the bridge.

What are some other reasons for charging tolls on roads and bridges?

Economics

Government Citizenship

Fast Fact 114

The *ZIP* in Zip Code stands for "Zone Improvement Plan."

What is the purpose of Zip Codes?

Fast Fact 115

Juneteenth celebrations began when Texas slaves learned of their freedom, two months after the end of the Civil War.

What is the name of the document President Lincoln signed that freed the slaves in Confederate states?

Culture

Geography

Fast Fact 116

Route 20 is the longest U.S. highway. This road begins in Boston, Massachusetts, runs through twelve states, and ends in Newport, Oregon.

Is Route 20 mostly an east-west or a north-south highway?

Fast Fact 117

King Ranch, an enormous cattle ranch in south Texas, is larger than the state of Rhode Island.

When did cattle drives begin in Texas?

History

Economics

Fast Fact 118

Banks around the world send money to each other 24 hours a day. Instead of cash, banks transmit computer messages giving the amount.

What can you do at an ATM, or automated teller machine?

Fast Fact 119

The Ohio state flag is the only state flag that isn't rectangular. It is shaped like a pennant.

How would you describe your state flag?

Government Citizenship

Culture

Fast Fact 120

In 1887 Oregon became the first state to recognize Labor Day as a holiday. Labor Day didn't become a national holiday until 1894.

What does Labor Day celebrate?

Fast Fact 121

Brooklyn **is Dutch for "Broken Valley."**

Brooklyn is part of what city?

Geography

History

Fast Fact 122

"Buffalo Bill" Cody and "Wild Bill" Hickok were both riders with the Pony Express.

How long did it take the Pony Express to deliver mail from Missouri to California?

Fast Fact 123

Schools for the formal training of teachers were called normal schools. They were established in the U.S. in the 1830s.

How do people today prepare for a career as a teacher?

Economics

Government
Citizenship

Fast Fact 124

By order of Congress, the Library of Congress receives two copies of all copyrighted items.

What is the difference between a *patent* and a *copyright*?

Fast Fact 125

The original Olympic Games were held every four years in Greece from 776 B.C. to A.D. 394. The first modern Olympic Games took place in 1896.

What are your favorite events in the Olympic Games?

Culture

Geography

Fast Fact 126

Sweet! It took more than 1,700 pounds of chocolate to make the world's only life-sized chocolate moose, located in Scarborough, Maine.

What are the names of the state, country, and ocean that border Maine?

Fast Fact 127

The scene on the New Jersey state quarter shows George Washington crossing the Delaware River.

When did this scene take place?

History

Economics

Fast Fact 128

Nearly two million children worked more than twelve hours a day in 1876. Many of them worked in dangerous mines and factories.

What state was the first to pass laws forbidding child labor?

Fast Fact 129

On New Year's Day 1907, Teddy Roosevelt shook hands with 8,513 people at a White House reception.

What are two other things you know about Teddy Roosevelt?

Government
Citizenship

Culture

Fast Fact 130

A Native American chef at a hotel in Saratoga Springs, New York, invented potato chips in 1853. He called them Saratoga Chips.

What are some other foods that were first eaten in America?

Fast Fact 131

A record-breaking snowstorm in late December 2001 dropped more than seven feet of snow on Buffalo, New York, in just under a week.

What is the name of the lake southwest of Buffalo that helps create such huge snowstorms?

Geography

History

Fast Fact 132

The first skyscraper in the world was only ten stories tall. It was built in Chicago in 1885.

Who invented a steel-making process that made skyscrapers possible?

Fast Fact 133

During the Gilded Age, Americans who achieved wealth celebrated it as never before. Mrs. Stuyvesant Fish threw a dinner party to honor her dog, who arrived wearing a $15,000 diamond collar!

What are some inventions from the 1870s and 1880s?

Economics

Government
Citizenship

Fast Fact 134

Oliver Wendell Holmes is the oldest justice ever to serve on the Supreme Court. He retired at the age of 90.

How many justices serve on the Supreme Court?

Fast Fact 135

The Olympic flag displays interlocking blue, yellow, black, green, and red rings. The colors were chosen because they represent every nation's flag.

What are the colors of your state flag?

Culture

Geography

Fast Fact 136

The largest sculpture in the world is currently under construction in the Black Hills of South Dakota. It honors Chief Crazy Horse, a Lakota Sioux.

What heroes do you think deserve a memorial?

Fast Fact 137

In 1848 only seven Chinese people were known to be living in the San Francisco area. By 1852 more than 25,000 Chinese had arrived in the area.

What brought the Chinese to San Francisco?

History

Economics

Fast Fact 138

The Pony Express charged five dollars an ounce to send mail from St. Louis to San Francisco. After the Pony Express failed, mail cost only three cents per half-ounce through the U.S. mail.

How much does it cost today to send a letter through the U.S. mail?

Fast Fact 139

Franklin Roosevelt was related, by blood or marriage, to eleven other United States presidents.

Who are the two presidents who are the sons of previous presidents?

Government Citizenship

Culture

Fast Fact 140

Wearing a cowboy hat is not just a fashion statement. The wide brim gives shade from the sun and protection from the rain, and the high crown keeps the wearer's head cool.

What region of the United States is most often associated with cowboys?

Fast Fact 141

The economy of the state of California is larger than the economies of many world nations.

How large is California, and what is its rank in terms of area among other states?

Geography

Fast Fact 142

The Wright brothers' first successful airplane flight lasted only about 12 seconds and traveled 120 feet.

Name another famous inventor from the United States and describe the invention.

Fast Fact 143

President Millard Fillmore and his wife, Abigail, installed the White House's first bathtub, kitchen stove, and library. Abigail had to apply to Congress for the funding for the library.

Where does Congress get the money to pay for White House expenses?

Economics

Government
Citizenship

Fast Fact 144

The Secret Service first assumed responsibility for the protection of the President of the United States in 1902.

What happened in 1901 to change the security needs of the president?

Fast Fact 145

Chopsticks and soup spoons are the only utensils at a traditional Chinese table.

What are some Chinese foods that have become popular in the United States?

Culture

Geography

Fast Fact 146

There are 132 islands in the state of Hawaii. The smallest populated island is Niihau, which has an area of only 73 square miles.

On which island is Hawaii's capital, Honolulu, located?

Fast Fact 147

At the end of the twentieth century, the Summer Olympic Games had been cancelled only three times: in 1916, 1940, and 1944.

What world events caused these cancellations?

History

Economics

Fast Fact 148

About 85 percent of all families in the United States own at least one car, and 35 percent own two or more cars.

Who designed the world's first mass-produced, affordable car?

Fast Fact 149

Louis Brandeis became the first Jewish Supreme Court justice in 1916.

Name two other Supreme Court justices.

Government Citizenship

Culture

Fast Fact 150

It took fourteen years and one million dollars to complete the National Memorial at Mount Rushmore.

Whose faces are carved into Mount Rushmore?

Fast Fact 151

The Chicago River is the only river in the United States that flows backward. Engineers changed the direction of the river's flow in 1900.

What major river forms the western border of Illinois?

Geography

History

Fast Fact 152

Hawaii is the only state that was once an independent kingdom. King Kamehameha I established this kingdom in 1810.

What queen ruled Hawaii in the late 1800s?

Fast Fact 153

Americans spend more than $100 billion on fast food every year, which is more than they spend on movies, books, magazines, newspapers, videos, and recorded music combined.

Would you rather spend $5 on fast food or entertainment? Why?

Economics

Government
Citizenship

Fast Fact 154

President Rutherford B. Hayes had the first telephone installed in the White House in 1877. Herbert Hoover was the first president to have a phone at his desk.

What major events took place in the United States during Hoover's presidency?

Fast Fact 155

Rosie the Riveter inspired songs and posters during World War II, and now a national park is being built to honor the contributions of the women Rosie symbolized.

What are some contributions that these women made?

Culture

Geography

Fast Fact 156

The Commonwealth of Liberia was founded in Africa in 1838 as a home for former African American slaves.

Find Liberia on a map. What countries surround it?

Fast Fact 157

Benjamin Harrison was the first president to bring a Christmas tree inside the White House. He was also the first president to employ a woman while in office.

What man served as President of the United States both before and after Benjamin Harrison?

History

Economics

Fast Fact 158

By 1927 fifteen million Model T automobiles had been built.

When was the first Model T built?

Fast Fact 159

Calvin Coolidge refused to use the telephone during the entire time he was president.

What significant cultural events took place during Coolidge's presidency?

Government Citizenship

Culture

Fast Fact 160

Thursday is named after Thor, the Norse god of thunder.

From what planet do you think Saturday gets its name?

Fast Fact 161

The three most visited natural attractions in the United States are the Grand Canyon, Yellowstone National Park, and Niagara Falls.

In what regions are these natural attractions located?

Geography

History

Fast Fact 162

William Taft loved law even more than politics. After his presidency he served as Chief Justice of the Supreme Court from 1921 until just before his death in 1930.

Which branch of government includes the Supreme Court?

Fast Fact 163

President Ronald Reagan loved jellybeans so much that his frequent eating of the candies increased their sales during his presidency.

What can cause a product to become popular?

Economics

Government
Citizenship

Fast Fact 164

The White House is made up of the East Wing, the West Wing, and the Residence. There are 132 rooms, 35 bathrooms, and 3 elevators in the Residence alone.

What is the name of the wing where the president works?

Fast Fact 165

The Internet was developed by the Department of Defense in the late 1960s, and was called ARPANet. By 1981 just over 200 computers were connected to it.

Where can you go to connect to the Internet?

Culture

Geography

Fast Fact 166

Robert Fulton studied in Paris to be a painter, but he did not do very well. He turned to engineering and designed an experimental submarine.

The steamship he designed, the *Clermont*, carried people between what two cities in New York?

Fast Fact 167

In May 1986, as many as seven million people clasped hands from New York to Los Angeles to raise money for the nation's homeless. This event was officially called "Hands Across America."

People held protests to draw attention to many issues in the 1960s. What were some of these issues?

History

Economics

Fast Fact 168

In 1998 women owned between 25 percent and 33 percent of the world's businesses.

For what is business owner Madam C. J. Walker famous?

Fast Fact 169

President Eisenhower was the first president of all fifty states.

How many states were there when Truman was president?

Government
Citizenship

Culture

Fast Fact 170

In 1970 Sirimavo Bandaranaike was elected the first female prime minister in the world.

Who are some women leaders that you admire?

Fast Fact 171

Every morning, the sun's rays fall on Maine before any other state in the United States.

Why does this occur?

Geography

History

Fast Fact 172

With the gardeners away fighting in the war, President Woodrow Wilson used sheep to keep the White House lawns trimmed and tidy.

In which war were the gardeners fighting?

Fast Fact 173

Each year California produces more fruits, nuts, and vegetables, including more than 500 million pounds of garlic, than any other state.

What agricultural products are produced in your state?

Economics

Government
Citizenship

Fast Fact 174

In 1872 Victoria Woodhull became the first woman to run for President of the United States. She was also the first woman stockbroker.

Who was the first woman appointed to the Supreme Court?

Fast Fact 175

Cultures all over the world have developed string instruments, which can be played either by plucking or with a bow.

What are the names of three string instruments?

Culture

Geography

Fast Fact 176

Missouri and Tennessee are each surrounded by eight other states.

Name the state that is bordered by only one other state.

Fast Fact 177

At the end of the twentieth century, only twelve humans had set foot on the moon, and they were all American men.

Who was the first man to walk on the moon, and what did he say as he did so?

History

Economics

Fast Fact 178

In 1994 Bill Gates paid almost $31 million at auction for one of Leonardo da Vinci's notebooks.

For what is Leonardo da Vinci famous?

Fast Fact 179

Franklin D. Roosevelt was elected president four times. The law was changed, and no President of the United States can now serve more than two terms.

How was this law changed?

Government Citizenship

Culture

Fast Fact 180

The triathlon and tae-kwon-do were first introduced to the Olympics at the Sydney Games in 2000.

What city hosted the last Olympic Games?

Fast Facts Answers

1. Seattle, Washington
2. Columbus and his crew began claiming the lands of North America for Spain.
3. the date of mint, the value of the coin, and the words *Liberty, In God We Trust,* and *United States of America*
4. the Dutch
5. Horses enabled the Cheyenne to move quickly, and more often, over greater distances.
6. Answers will vary, but may include the Bahama, Bermuda, or Falkland Islands.
7. Answers may include Mesa Verde or the Four Corners region.
8. Answers will vary, but may include cooper, sailor, shoemaker, or blacksmith.
9. Answers may include American flag, bald eagle, Great Seal, or Uncle Sam.
10. Answers may include the Aztec, Maya, and Inca, as well as the Hopewell, Mississippian, and Adena peoples.
11. New Mexico in the Southwest
12. Answers may include glass jars and bottles, alminum cans, plastic containers, and so on.
13. a portrait of George Washington
14. Answers will vary.
15. the Aztecs
16. Answers will vary, but may include the Mojave or Great Salt Lake Deserts.
17. Francisco Pizarro, a Spaniard
18. Commemorative coins are produced in smaller number and are collectible. Both commemorative and circulating coins are legal tender.
19. Senate and House of Representatives
20. Answers may include porcelain, chopsticks, pasta, paper money, or silk.
21. Mt. McKinley, Alaska
22. the Revolutionary War
23. Answers will vary.
24. Answer will depend on state.
25. the Aztec ruler Montezuma

26. Russia
27. 1920
28. in the colony of Virginia
29. Answer will depend on year.
30. Answers will vary, but may include Lent or Passover.
31. Niagara Falls, American Falls, or Horseshoe Falls
32. Georgia
33. Only the national government is allowed to determine what may be issued as currency.
34. Answers will depend on state.
35. They were in territory controlled by Spain.
36. the Missouri River
37. Revere was one of three men to warn the people of Concord that the British were on the way to seize military supplies.
38. slaves
39. France
40. Answers will vary.
41. in Northern California
42. nylon or silk (may have been hemp in WWII)
43. penny, nickel, dime, quarter, half dollar, silver dollar, gold dollar
44. Answer will depend on state.
45. the United States
46. Alaska
47. Sacagawea
48. Massachusetts raised taxes to pay its war debt. Shays's Rebellion arose to demand lower taxes and close the courts that punished debtors.
49. The Constitution requires a census; it is used to determine representation in the House, and to allocate some government funds.
50. It marks the signing of the Declaration of Independence in 1776.
51. Answers may include the Battles of Trenton, Princeton, or Monmouth.
52. the Seneca, Cayuga, Onondaga, Oneida, and Tuscarora
53. John Hancock

54. Answers may include that he helped write the Declaration of Independence and the Constitution.
55. walrus or hippopotamus teeth, and possibly some of his own teeth
56. the Atlantic Ocean
57. Answers will vary, but may include prime minister, czar, or queen.
58. paper bills called "Continentals," paper money from a particular state, foreign coins
59. in 1788
60. Answers may include, among others, staying up late or eating special foods.
61. Chicago
62. Answers will vary, but may include that he was the second president or that he was a Federalist.
63. Robert Fulton
64. Washington, D.C.
65. Answers will vary, but may include using proper titles, listening well, or being polite.
66. the Columbia River in Washington state
67. the War of 1812
68. Manufactured goods could be shipped from eastern factories to the Midwest, and Midwestern farm products could be shipped in the opposite direction.
69. Answers may include books, recordings of music, videos, and so on.
70. Answers will vary.
71. Illinois, Kentucky, Tennessee, Arkansas, Oklahoma, Kansas, Nebraska, and Iowa
72. *U.S.S. Constitution,* also known as "Old Ironsides"
73. railroads
74. He had written and signed the Declaration of Independence, been part of the Continental Congress, invented a great many useful items, and helped create a great nation.
75. People who came to California in 1849 to mine for gold were called 49ers.
76. Jefferson City, MO; Madison, WI; Lincoln, NE
77. Morse Code
78. coins

79. Answers will vary, but may include to track the rise or fall of industries, or to determine allocations of funds or services.
80. Swahili
81. 360 miles
82. 1820s: ME, MO; 1830s: AR, MI, FL; 1840s: TX, IA, WI, CA; 1850s: MN, OR; 1860s: KS, WV, NV, NE; 1870s: CO
83. Answers will vary, but may include the inventions of the cotton gin and reaper, and improved transportation to bring product to larger markets.
84. G. Washington, J. Adams, T. Jefferson, J. Madison, J. Monroe, J. Q. Adams, A. Jackson
85. Answers will vary, but may include that the food is a leading industry, or that it marks a certain time of year.
86. the Santa Fe, Oregon, and California Trails
87. Answers will vary, but may include Lucretia Mott or Sojourner Truth.
88. taxes
89. thirteen
90. about 30
91. Mississippi, Missouri, and Big Sioux Rivers
92. Andrew Johnson
93. Answers may indicate that a $1 bill is used more often.
94. Texas
95. Answers may include New Year's Day, Veterans Day, Dr. Martin Luther King, Jr.'s Birthday, Memorial Day, Independence Day, Labor Day, Columbus Day, and Thanksgiving.
96. Superior, Michigan, Huron, Erie, Ontario
97. California
98. Answers may include doctor, dentist, researcher, and so on.
99. Answers should indicate prevention of counterfeiting.
100. Answers will vary.
101. the Rocky Mountains
102. the California Trail

103. Answers may include to demand better wages, an 8-hour workday, or safer working conditions.
104. Answers will vary, but may include setting up a sorting system or placing containers in recycling instead of trash.
105. Answers may include, among others, e-mail, telephone, or letters.
106. Lake Mead
107. *Uncle Tom's Cabin*, the Civil War
108. the telegraph
109. Answer will depend on the year.
110. Answers will vary.
111. the Hawaiian Islands
112. about 25
113. Answers will vary, but may include to pay for road improvements, or to control traffic.
114. They are used by the Post Office to deliver mail more efficiently.
115. the Emancipation Proclamation

116. east-west
117. in the 1860s
118. withdraw money or carry out other banking procedures by inserting an encoded plastic card
119. Answers will vary.
120. It honors the contributions of workers in the United States.
121. New York City
122. ten days
123. through college courses and classroom training
124. Copyrights protect the production, use, and sale of creative efforts such as books, music, and software, for a set number of years; patents protect inventions the same way.
125. Answers will vary.
126. New Hampshire, Canada, the Atlantic Ocean
127. December 25, 1776
128. Massachusetts

129. Answers will vary, but may include that the Teddy Bear was named after him or that he was the twenty-sixth president.
130. Answers will vary, but may include hot dogs, corn, or waffle cones.
131. Lake Erie
132. Henry Bessemer
133. Answers may include the telephone, automobile, and electric lights, among others.
134. nine
135. Answers will vary.
136. Answers will vary.
137. the Gold Rush
138. Answer will depend on year.
139. John Quincy Adams and George W. Bush
140. the West
141. 155,973 square miles; third largest state
142. Answers will vary, but may include Edison (electric light bulb, phonograph, movie camera), Latimer (long-lasting light bulb), or Sholes (typewriter).
143. taxes
144. President McKinley was assassinated.
145. Answers may include egg rolls, fortune cookies, pot stickers, dumplings, and so on.
146. Oahu
147. World Wars I and II
148. Henry Ford
149. Answers will vary.
150. the faces of Presidents Washington, Jefferson, T. Roosevelt, and Lincoln
151. the Mississippi River
152. Queen Liliuokalani
153. Answers will vary.
154. the stock market crash and the beginning of the Great Depression
155. They went to work in factories and built warships and airplanes.
156. Sierra Leone, Guinea, and the Ivory Coast (or Côte d'Ivoire)
157. Grover Cleveland
158. 1908

159. Answers may include Lindbergh's flight across the Atlantic, the rise of the Jazz Age, or the first *talkies*.
160. the planet Saturn
161. The Grand Canyon is in the Southwest, Yellowstone is in the West, and Niagara Falls is in the Northeast.
162. the judicial branch
163. Answers will vary, but may include endorsement by a popular figure, usefulness, or quality of the item.
164. the West Wing
165. Answers may include home, classroom, or public or school library, among others.
166. New York City and Albany
167. Answers will vary, but may include civil rights, equal rights for women, farm worker safety, or the war in Vietnam.
168. She was the first African American woman millionaire.
169. forty-eight

170. Answers will vary, but may include Golda Meir, Joan of Arc, Eleanor Roosevelt, or the First Lady.
171. Maine is the easternmost state.
172. World War I
173. Answers will vary.
174. Sandra Day O'Connor
175. Answers may include, among others, violin, guitar, and mandolin.
176. Maine
177. Neil Armstrong; "That's one small step for man . . . one giant leap for mankind."
178. He is famous as a painter, sculptor, architect, engineer, and scientist. He kept notebooks of his drawings and ideas for machines.
179. by an amendment to the Constitution
180. Answer will depend on year.